W9-AWM-916

WONDERS OF THE WORLD

The Grand Canyon

Other books in the Wonders of the World series include:

Gems
Geysers
Icebergs
Mummies
Quicksand

917.91
KAL

24692

WONDERS OF THE WORLD

The Grand Canyon

Stuart A. Kallen

**KIDHAVEN
PRESS™**

THOMSON
™
GALE

San Diego • Detroit • New York • San Francisco • Cleveland
New Haven, Conn. • Waterville, Maine • London • Munich

© 2003 by KidHaven Press. KidHaven Press is an imprint of The Gale Group, Inc.,
a division of Thomson Learning, Inc.

KidHaven™ and Thomson Learning™ are trademarks used herein under license.

For more information, contact
KidHaven Press
27500 Drake Rd.
Farmington Hills, MI 48331-3535
Or you can visit our Internet site at http://www.gale.com

ALL RIGHTS RESERVED.
No part of this work covered by the copyright hereon may be reproduced or used in any form
or by any means—graphic, electronic, or mechanical, including photocopying, recording,
taping, Web distribution or information storage retrieval systems—without the written
permission of the publisher.

LIBRARY OF CONGRESS CATALOGING-IN-PUBLICATION DATA

Kallen, Stuart A., 1955–
   The Grand Canyon / by Stuart A. Kallen.
      p. cm. — (Wonders of the world)
Summary: Discusses how the Grand Canyon was formed, its early exploration, and
the plants and animals found there.
Includes bibliographical references and index.
   ISBN 0-7377-1488-3 (lib. bdg. : alk. paper)
   1. Grand Canyon (Ariz.)—Juvenile literature. [1. Grand Canyon (Ariz.)]
   I. Title. II. Wonders of the world
   F788 .K35 2003
   917.91'32—dc21

                          2002013062

Printed in the United States of America

CONTENTS

The Making of the Grand Canyon

The Grand Canyon is one of the most amazing natural wonders in the world. Almost everything about the canyon inspires awe. Located in the northwestern corner of Arizona, this gigantic crack in the earth is 277 miles long, 18 miles wide in some places, and averages more than 1 mile deep. The beauty of the canyon is spectacular. Towering **buttes**, flat-topped **mesas**, and deep gorges glitter by day beneath a turquoise-blue sky. And these rocks reveal more colors than a box of crayons with infinite shades of red, pink, purple, green, gold, blue, brown, black, silver, and white. Some of these remarkable rocks are ancient—1.7 billion years old, or 17 million centuries—half the age of Earth itself. But the canyon itself is new by comparison.

The Grand Canyon was carved slowly and steadily over the past 6 million years by the powerful flowing wa-

The rainbow-colored Grand Canyon is a breathtaking,
natural landscape.

ters of the Colorado River, and by smaller streams—known as **tributaries**—that flow into it. The Colorado River performed this extraordinary work of nature by washing sand, mud, and gravel—debris known as **sediment**—along its course. For millions of years, the river carried a daily average of about five hundred thousand tons of sediment, a massive amount that would fill one hundred thousand large dump trucks every twenty-four hours. This sediment acted as sandpaper, gradually **eroding**, or deepening, the canyon about six inches every one thousand years.

Rising Plates

Another force of nature—more powerful than the Colorado River—is also at work in the Grand Canyon. This process, called **uplift**, happens when huge pieces of land, known as plates, move over Earth's inner core of molten lava. These plates slowly rub into, crash against, and dive under one another. When this happens over millions of years, continents such as North America are formed. Mountains are pushed up and ocean basins are formed.

The rim of the canyon, known as the Colorado **Plateau**, has been pushed upward as a result of this movement. The landmass lies on top of the North American plate, which was once under the ocean and is now as high as nine thousand feet above sea level in some places. This process continues, even today, as the Colorado Plateau is pushed even higher while the Colorado River carves the Grand Canyon deeper into the earth.

As the Grand Canyon was sliced into the ground, layers of rock were exposed that show nearly 2 billion

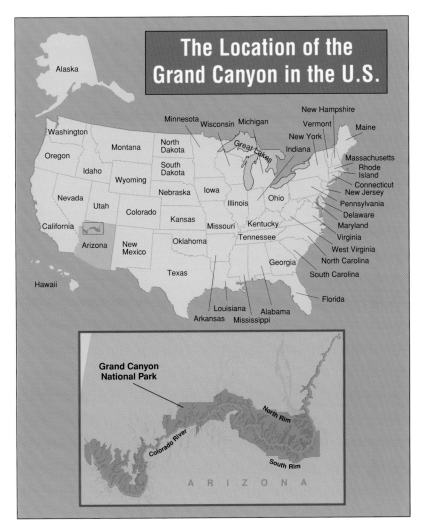

years of Earth's history. Those who study the origin, history, and structure of Earth are known as **geologists**. These scientists can read the various rock layers like a book, learning about the natural formation of the Grand Canyon.

The oldest rock in the Grand Canyon is the hard granite at the bottom where the Colorado River flows. This ancient pink, blue, gray, and black stone was once molten lava spit out of Earth's core by volcanoes. Above the granite are different layers of younger stone, known as sedimentary rock, because they are composed of sediment. These rocks include limestone, sandstone, and shale.

Limestone is made of the remains of the bones, teeth, and shells of ancient sea animals. In fact, a close inspection of the limestone will show the remains of these creatures imbedded in the rock. The presence of limestone tells scientists that the Grand Canyon region was under an ocean long ago.

As the ocean dried up, it left behind shale, a type of rock made from dried mud. Various minerals color this shale and help add to the canyon's glorious color scheme. After the ocean vanished completely, sandy desert was left behind. This is revealed by the canyon sandstone—rock made from compressed sand.

The layered sedimentary rocks erode at different rates. This makes the canyon walls a fascinating jumble of stairways, ledges, and jagged rock formations carved by wind, rain, and water. Because the limestone is harder than the other sedimentary rocks, it makes sheer cliffs in the canyon walls. Sandstone and shale are more prone to erosion, and so they leave behind gentle sloping walls. In some places limestone juts out several feet over worn layers of sandstone and shale layers.

Stories Told by Fossils

Fossils—the stonelike remains of ancient plants and animals—reveal what sort of creatures lived in the canyon at various times. The Grand Canyon contains millions of fossils, and geologists can tell the history of a specific rock layer by the types of fossils it contains. For example, the gray-white limestone seen on the upper levels of the canyon is

Layers of sedimentary rock look like stripes in the bright Arizona sun.

layered with clam like brachiopods, coral, mollusks, and sea lilies, that lived here 250 million years ago. The sandstone below it, 260 million years old, contains the footprints of reptiles, proving that the area was previously a desert.

Lower down, shale formed 265 million years ago contains fossils of ferns, pine trees, and amphibians such as frogs. This tells geologists that the area was once a forest where abundant rain fell.

Further down the canyon purplish limestone forms massive cliffs hundreds of feet high. This stone contains fossils of fish that lived in a freshwater lake 335 million years ago. These fossils show geologists that although the

A trilobite is one of many fossils buried in the ancient rock of the Grand Canyon.

Grand Canyon may be hundreds of miles from the ocean today, the area was at one time underwater, deprived of water, and even a tropical lakeside paradise. And no one knows what it will be 1 million years from now.

The Canyon Today

The ancient rock walls of the Grand Canyon appear little different than they did centuries ago. But man-made changes in the last fifty years have drastically altered the flow of the Colorado River, as well as the canyon that depends on this life-giving source of water. The Glen Canyon Dam, built upstream from the Grand Canyon in 1963, has reduced the amount of water flowing into the Colorado River by 80 to 95 percent. This dam has stopped the river from carrying the daily five hundred thousand tons of sediment that it once did.

The Glen Canyon Dam changed the natural ecology of the Grand Canyon. Where spring floodwaters once scoured the canyon walls and deposited sandbars along the banks, the river was tamed. In some places the low flow of the river has allowed sediment deposited from tributaries to fill in the channel rather than cut it deeper, as it had for millions of years.

Despite these changes the Grand Canyon remains a natural wonder. And the giant trench in the earth continues to attract more than 5 million visitors a year to Grand Canyon National Park. The park includes more than 1 million acres of land that is part of the canyon. While dams and parks may cause changes to the Grand Canyon, these are temporary. The Colorado River has been cutting into the earth for 6 million years, while the Glen Canyon

The building of the Glen Canyon Dam (pictured) has changed the natural balance of the Grand Canyon.

Dam is expected to last another two hundred. Long after the dam is gone, geologists are sure that the river will continue to shape and sculpt the Grand Canyon for millions of years into the future.

The Grand Voyage

The Grand Canyon was largely unexplored when it became part of the United States in 1848. And it was not until 1869 that anyone was brave enough—or some say foolish enough—to attempt to navigate the Colorado River through the canyon. At that time a Civil War veteran named John Wesley Powell assembled a team of eight seasoned war veterans and frontiersmen to sail the entire 277-mile length of the canyon.

Powell, who had lost his right arm in a Civil War battle, was a professor of geology when he undertook the difficult and dangerous journey. In order to navigate the canyon, Powell designed and built four special boats, and then transported them from Chicago to Wyoming by train.

Three of the oak boats were twenty-one feet long and weighed nearly one thousand pounds each. They had built-in

John Wesley Powell made the grueling journey down the Colorado River in 1869.

watertight compartments that Powell hoped would prevent them from sinking in the turbulent waters. These compartments were also used to stow up to two thousand pounds of provisions and equipment needed for the long journey. Each boat was meant to be rowed by two crew members. The fourth boat, sixteen feet long and built of pine, was fast and light and was used by Powell for scouting.

With limited space, Powell chose the equipment carefully, bringing guns and ammunition, traps for catching small animals, food, kegs of whiskey, and tools for boat repair. In addition, the professor brought scientific instruments such as sextants and compasses for navigating, barometers for measuring river elevation, and thermometers to record weather and water conditions. The food and equipment were divided among the three boats so that if one sank, the team would not be stranded. Powell's scouting boat did not carry food.

Risky Rapids

The Powell **expedition** began its journey on May 24, 1869, at the Green River, which flows into the Colorado. As the group sailed downstream, they named various landmarks, such as Flaming Gorge, where they survived their first series of rapids. The joy of this early success, however, quickly faded as the crew faced a seemingly endless series of dangerous rapids and waterfalls caused by steep descents in the riverbed.

A kayaker meets the dangerous rapids of the Colorado River as it flows through the middle of the canyon.

These churning chutes of white water flowing over, under, and between sharp, jagged boulders forced the expedition to invent different methods for moving the boats down the river. In some places, the crews could not simply navigate their vessels with paddles and rudders. Instead, they were forced to unload the boats and carry tons of equipment downstream on their backs. Then they had to guide the empty boats downstream with long ropes—all the while slipping, sliding, and falling on muddy riverbanks.

Some parts of the river were so hazardous that even this difficult and time-consuming method did not work. In an area known as Lodore Canyon, swift rapids and waterfalls forced the men to take the boats out of the water and roll them over the jagged, hilly shoreline on driftwood logs.

Serious Disaster

On June 9, the Powell expedition ran into its first serious disaster when attempting to navigate a dangerous stretch of white water. One boat was shattered into splinters on a set of rocks, which the group immediately named Disaster Falls. The crew was lucky enough to be washed onto a small island in the middle of the river where they had to be rescued by the other men. This event was not good for the crew's morale. Only three weeks into their journey, and one of their boats, along with one-third of their provisions, were lost. And this brush with death was enough to scare off one crew member, Frank Goodman, who left after losing everything he owned in the rapids.

Finally, on August 5, after weeks of death-defying experiences sailing, dragging, and sliding their remaining boats downstream, the Powell team sailed into Marble

Canyon at the northernmost section of today's Grand Canyon National Park.

A Hard Row to Go

Although the scenery was breathtaking, by the time the Powell expedition entered the Grand Canyon the crew was trying to simply survive. The men were soaking wet all the time, their boats needed almost endless repairs, and the crew was forced to frequently carve new oars from driftwood to replace those that had been shattered by

John Wesley Powell poses with Chief Tav-Gu of the Painte Indians during his Colorado River expedition.

rocks. And the harsh climate of the canyon provided little comfort. By day the men were baked under a merciless sun, and at night chilly winds blew sand in their faces. On windless nights, huge clouds of bloodsucking mosquitoes rose from the riverbanks to torment the exhausted men. And they had little resistance to the maddening insects. Their clothes had been ripped to shreds by rocks and bushes, and their ponchos and blankets were lost in the turbulent rapids. Rain only added to the misery. At one point, a weeklong rainstorm prevented the group from advancing more than two miles in seven days.

As the expedition continued into the Grand Canyon, food supplies were short and the men existed on coffee, dried apples, and biscuits made from moldy flour. When the canyon walls got higher, the river narrower, and the rapids steeper and longer, the men grew more frightened and depressed. At any minute, without warning, the river could turn into a deadly whirlpool of rapids, logs, and boulders. And conditions continued to worsen.

By August 24, the food was gone, but luckily conditions began to improve. On August 29, the Powell expedition passed out of the Grand Canyon at Grand Wash Cliffs. With this passage, they became the first known men to have boated down the Colorado River through the Grand Canyon. At this point, Powell and his brother Richard left the expedition while the remaining group continued down the Colorado to its end at the Gulf of California.

Following Powell into the Canyon

After the expedition, John Powell was hailed as a national hero. In 1870 he published *New Tracks in North America*,

The Colorado River winds through the Grand Canyon. John Powell became a national hero after being the first to boat down the river.

his account of the grueling journey. Powell attempted several more runs through the canyon in later years, though these trips were unsuccessful and marked by one disaster after another.

In the following years, few people were brave enough to imitate Powell's record-setting trip through the Grand Canyon. By 1954 only two hundred people had made the journey. But the availability of large rubber rafts after World War II made it easier for people to travel the canyon. Today, tens of thousands of white-water rafters run the Colorado rapids through the Grand Canyon every year. The colorful towering cliffs continue to inspire awe while the swirling rapids provide excitement and danger to those who raft through the spectacular canyon.

CHAPTER THREE

Plants of the Grand Canyon

As John Wesley Powell and his crew discovered, the environment within the Grand Canyon is harsh and unforgiving. Extreme temperatures, dry desert conditions, and great changes in elevation mean only the strongest survive within its boundaries. Despite this, the Grand Canyon is home to more than fifteen hundred **species** of plants.

The elevation of the Grand Canyon ranges from twelve hundred feet above sea level at the Colorado River to ninety-one hundred feet on the North Rim. At the lower elevations, the climate is like that of a desert. At the higher reaches of the canyon, the weather can be more like that of Canada or even the Arctic Circle.

Within this nearly eight-thousand-foot difference in elevation, special areas, called "life zones" by biologists, support a wide variety of plant life. And within each life zone are several mini-**ecosystems** or subzones. These smaller zones are shaped by their own specific weather conditions, called microclimates. For example, part of one zone may face south and is hot and dry. Yet another part of the same zone may be wet and cool because it faces north. These conditions determine what types of plants and animals live within each area of the canyon.

In the harsh Upper Zone of the Grand Canyon scraggly plants grow among dry rocks.

The Lower Sonoran Zone

The lowest reaches of the Grand Canyon are called the Lower Sonoran Zone. Here, the climate is dry and desert-like. Temperatures can vary from 110°F during the day to 30°F to 40°F at night. Only plants that need very little water—and those that store liquids for long periods of time—can live here. Cacti are the most common plants of this type.

Short, stout barrel cacti can live in the lowest elevations of the canyon because these plants have long root systems to soak up large amounts of water from rain and dew. The roots deliver the liquid for storage in the sponge-like tissues within the cactus. Hundreds of razor-sharp needles prevent water-seeking animals from nibbling on the barrel.

Cacti such as the desert prickly pear and the beavertail cactus survive in a similar manner. These cacti flower in the spring and bear brightly colored fruit in the late summer. Native Americans have traditionally made jams and syrups from the sweet cactus fruit.

Seeking and Saving Water

The canyon floor also supports other common desert species such as sagebrush, manzanita, and yucca. These plants have special leaves that are hairy, waxy, or very small, a survival technique that prevents water loss from wind and sun. When rain does fall in the inner canyon, grasses sprout, and delicate flowers such as columbines and monkey flowers pop up along canyon walls.

Other plants rely on river water or spring water for survival. Rafters on the river often see bright green Fre-

This bright prickly pear cactus flower blooms during the spring in the Lower Sonoran Zone.

mont cottonwood trees shimmering on sandy beaches, along with pink-flowered tamarisk and graceful willows. These thirsty trees sink roots into the river and have a steady source of liquid nourishment.

Unlike the cottonwood and tamarisk, mesquite bushes may live far from the riverbanks. These bushes survive in the driest areas because of their long water-seeking roots.

One mesquite bush was found to have a root system that tunneled down 175 feet to find water deep underground.

The Upper Zone

The area of the Grand Canyon between the elevation of about thirty-five hundred feet and seven thousand feet is called the Upper Sonoran Zone. This area has a wide variety of climates that include plants that live in the desert, mountain, and grassland.

Flowering plants such as the cliff rose and fern bush—shrubs related to the rose family—add splendor and color to the Upper Sonoran Zone. The cliff rose has twisted, gnarled branches that are not known for their beauty. But when late winter rains fall, the bush sprouts sweet-smelling white flowers that attract bees and birds. The delicate, bright red flowers of the Utah penstemon may be seen along the rocky terrain, while carmine thistles grow nearby.

The higher elevations of the Upper Sonoran Zone, between four thousand feet and sixty-five hundred feet, is a subzone known as the Mountain Shrub Area. Winter temperatures may drop below zero and summer temperatures may top out at 110°F. In this climate, deciduous bushes, those that lose their leaves in the winter, survive drastic annual temperature changes. These plants include scrub and wavyleaf oak, along with New Mexican locust, a shrubby plant that sprouts fragrant pink flowers in June. Berries also grow in the Mountain Shrub Area, with snowberry, barberry, and serviceberry providing fruit for hungry birds, rabbits, squirrels, and other animals.

A glistening waterfall is a rare sight in the desert environment of the Grand Canyon.

The Transition Zone

The area around the canyon rim, between sixty-five hundred feet and eight thousand feet, is known as the Transition Zone. In this area, the grasslands and deserts disappear as forests dominate the scenery. In the lower levels of the Transition Zone, thick forests of piñon pine and Utah juniper mix with cliff rose and sagebrush. The trees in this area, called the piñon-juniper woodland, are small and stunted as a result of poor soil and lack of moisture.

While the piñon never grows more than thirty feet high, it is hardy and can survive for more than four hundred years in the dry, rocky soil. And for centuries the nuts of the piñon cone have been an important food source for Native Americans in the region.

In the higher elevations of the Transition Zone, Gambel oak and ponderosa pine rule the skyline. Ponderosa pines may be up to six hundred years old and grow to a height of one hundred feet on the South and North Rims, where they thrive with the extra moisture provided by winter snowfall. The ponderosas are beloved for their fragrant bark that some say smells like vanilla, caramel, or cinnamon.

The climate of the Transition Zone allows for a variety of wildflowers that sprout in the area in summer and fall. White baby asters, yellow sunflowers, golden western wallflowers, Indian paintbrush, purple hill lupine, and others provide a rainbow of color throughout the rim area.

The Highest Zones

The highest elevations of the Grand Canyon region, called the Boreal Zone, support plant life that would commonly be

Riders on mules journey high up into the forested Boreal Zone.

seen in Canada or even above Hudson Bay near the Arctic Circle. This zone is found only on the north side of the Colorado River in the area known as the Kaibab Plateau between elevations of eight thousand feet and ninety-one hundred feet.

Visitors to the Boreal Zone can see Douglas fir, white fir, and quaking aspen commonly found in mountain regions of the West. On the forest floor between the trees,

The snowy upper elevations of the Grand Canyon contrast with the dry landscape beneath.

hardy mountain plants such as gooseberry, wild rose, and wormwood may be found. More sun shines on the flattest areas of the Kaibab Plateau. There, mountain grasslands and meadows are rife with wildflowers such as giant hyssop, bellflower, bluebell, buttercup, sheep sorrel, and goldenrod.

From the cool, moist upper elevations of the park down to the hot, dry river region one mile below the rim, the Grand Canyon is home to thousands of plant species. To view these plants anywhere else, a traveler would have to walk from the deserts of Mexico to the Arctic Circle— a distance of nearly three thousand miles. But a hike down the steep canyon paths takes a visitor through dozens of climate zones and subzones in a single day. And the beauty of the plant life found within those zones is yet another reason that this amazing canyon is so grand.

Animals of the Grand Canyon

Between the towering cliffs, frigid mountains, blazing deserts, and cold rivers, the Grand Canyon provides **habitat** for a wide variety of animal life. Ecosystems within the canyon support at least seventy-five species of mammals, fifty species of reptiles and amphibians, twenty species of fish, and more than three hundred types of birds. And each one of these animals has developed special survival skills to live within the rugged canyon environment.

Animals within the Grand Canyon range from common squirrels and chipmunks to exotic bobcats and mountain lions. Some of the animals may be found in populated tourist areas, while others exist in the most remote sections of the canyon. Wherever they live, most of these animals have to struggle with weather, terrain, and sometimes fierce predators to survive.

A bobcat waits for the right moment to leap upon its prey.

Swimming in the River

The deep green waters of the Colorado often flash silver as sunlight glints off the backs of the many fish that live within the river. But while many fish thrive here, only eight species are native to the Grand Canyon. All other types of fish were stocked in the river by humans.

The native fish include several species of chub including the humpbacked, bonytail, and roundtail chub, which can grow up to fifteen inches long. Suckers, such as the flannelmouth, razorback, and bluehead, reach up to two feet in length and weigh several pounds. The Colorado squawfish is perhaps the most interesting of the native fish, growing up to five feet long and weighing up to eighty pounds.

Squawfish and other native species have been seriously harmed, however, by the construction of the Glen Canyon Dam and Lake Powell. Before the dam was built, water temperature in the Colorado River changed with the seasons, reaching as high as 80°F in the summer. Today, the water flowing out of Lake Powell is cold, no warmer than 42°F to 49°F year-round. Many fish, such as the chub, that survive in warm water, struggle in the cold.

Native fish are also threatened by about fifteen nonnative species such as bullhead, catfish, and various types of trout including rainbow, cutthroat, brown, and brook that have been stocked in the river over the decades. Today, about 90 percent of the fish found in the canyon are nonnative species.

Leaping Lizards

While fish habitat has been drastically altered, little has changed for the cold-blooded reptiles that live in the sizzling, sun-drenched lower elevations of the Grand Canyon. Geckos—three-inch, yellow-and-brown-striped lizards—earned their name because they make a clicking noise that sounds like "gecko." While geckos may be seen darting about at night climbing up rocks in search of bugs, worms, and spiders, their little bodies cannot stand temperatures any higher than 84°F. As a result, geckos spend the days hidden under yucca plants and clinging to the underside of logs waiting for the sun to set.

While geckos shun the heat, the western chuckwalla thrives in temperatures hovering around 110°F and is seen

The gecko is an uncommon sight during the heat of the day.

only on the hottest afternoons. With a body length of eight inches and an additional ten-inch tail, the chuckwalla is the largest of the fifteen lizard species in the canyon. Chuckwallas are vegetarians, living on flowers and leaves, but they cannot drink water. Instead, they obtain all the moisture they need from their food. Because vegetation within the canyon absorbs so much salt from the soil, chuckwallas have extremely high sodium diets. But these large lizards have salt-removal glands in their nostrils. When they sneeze, they shoot streams of salt crystals out of their noses.

One of the smaller lizards within the Grand Canyon is the zebra-tailed lizard—only 3.5 inches long. But this little creature is one of the fastest animals of any sort within the park. When it feels threatened it can stand up on its hind legs and run away at speeds of up to eighteen miles per hour.

Majestic Birds

Lizards are among the many food sources for birds within the Grand Canyon. But most birds that live in the lower elevations are waterfowl that hunt and fish along the Colorado River.

Sandpipers may be seen on the banks of the river, bobbing along while snatching flying insects out of the air. Colorful birds such as swifts, warblers, swallows, and goldfinches build their nests in dense brush that grows along the riverbanks. And the river itself provides a perfect fishing ground for cormorants, great blue herons, and other waterfowl. Swans, geese, and mallards are bird tourists who stop along the river while migrating south in the autumn and north in the spring.

The red-tailed hawk is one of many predatory birds found at the Grand Canyon.

The craggy walls and open skies over the canyon attract many predatory birds such as hawks, falcons, and eagles. The red-tailed hawk is the most common, soaring high above the cliffs and plateaus in search of a rodent or rabbit meal.

One of the most majestic birds in the canyon, the golden eagle, nests high in the sheer cliff walls. With a six-foot wingspan, this super predator can carry off squirrels, fish, and even baby bighorn sheep.

The rarest bird in the canyon is the California condor, the largest bird in North America. Once nearly extinct, these birds, with ten-foot wingspans, have been reestablished in the park after three breeding pairs were released in 1996.

In the highest elevations of the park, the great horned owl may be heard hooting in the pine forests. These creatures hunt only at night and fly silently through the dark. They capture many mammal and bird species, including rabbits, mice, squirrels, ducks, and grouse, by swooping down and grabbing them with their razor-sharp talons.

Magnificent Mammals

Mice, squirrels, and rabbits are common within the canyon ecosystem and provide food for birds. However, many large mammals also make their home within the park. Mule deer are a common sight along highways and trails, while bighorn sheep live on only the most isolated slopes of the inner canyon. The sheep are able to leap nearly straight up rocky cliffs to escape danger. In the spring, males may be seen in head-butting contests, cracking their large horns together to determine who will mate with the females.

The most fearsome predators are mountain lions, which grow up to eight feet in length and weigh up to 275 pounds. Also known as cougars, pumas, and panthers, these carnivorous (meat-eating) creatures are found throughout the park and have been known to stalk and kill human beings on rare occasions. Although this is rare, mountain lions will eat other large creatures, such as many deer and elk found within the lion's habitat.

The elk that provide a feast for the mountain lion are regal creatures found in the forest rims of the canyon. Elk can weigh up to 750 pounds, and their huge, spreading antlers are used for head-butting duels in the spring. Elk, like mountain lions and bighorn sheep, were once hunted

A bighorn sheep balances on a rocky cliff edge.

A mountain lion is one of the most ferocious predators living in the Grand Canyon.

to near extinction. Today they are protected within the park and their numbers are increasing.

While the most common animal in the Grand Canyon today is the human being, birds, fish, lizards, and mammals have lived here for billions of years. With its million-acre roadless wilderness and harsh, inhospitable terrain, the Grand Canyon remains one of the last untouched wilderness areas in North America.

Glossary

buttes: Hills that rise abruptly from the surrounding area and have sloping sides and a flat top.

ecosystems: Communities of plants and animals functioning together within their environment.

eroding: Wearing away of rock or soil by water, wind, or ice.

expedition: A journey undertaken by a group of people with a specific goal, such as exploring the Grand Canyon for scientific purposes.

fossils: Remains of ancient organisms such as skeletons or leaf imprints that are embedded and preserved in rock.

geologists: Scientists who study the origin, history, and structure of Earth.

habitat: A specific environment in which an organism or group of organisms normally lives.

mesas: Broad, flat-topped hills with steep sides.

plateau: An elevated, level expanse of land also known as tableland.

sediment: Solid fragments of dirt, mud, and gravel that come from the weathering of rock and are carried by wind, water, or ice.

species: A category or type of plant or animal.

tributaries: Streams that flow into a larger river.

uplift: The natural process that raises or lifts large areas of land such as the Colorado Plateau around the rim of the Grand Canyon.

For Further Exploration

Books

Lynne Foster, *Exploring the Grand Canyon: Adventures of Yesterday and Today*. Grand Canyon, AZ: Grand Canyon Natural History Association, 1990. The natural and human history of the Grand Canyon with information about hiking, drawing, and other activities.

Wendell Minor, *Grand Canyon: Exploring a Natural Wonder*. New York: Blue Sky Press, 1998. Watercolor pictures and text by the author highlight the subtle beauty of the canyon.

David Petersen, *Grand Canyon National Park*. New York: Childrens Press, 2001. This book about the Grand Canyon focuses on the area within the national park.

Linda Vieira, *Grand Canyon: A Trail Through Time*. New York: Walker, 1997. Describes the geological history that may be seen in the walls of the Grand Canyon by hiking on trails in the national park.

Aileen Weintraub, *The Grand Canyon: The Widest Canyon*. New York: PowerKids Press, 2001. Part of the Great Record Breakers in Nature series, the text focuses on the most amazing facts about the canyon, illustrated with beautiful photographs.

Website

The National Park Service (www.nps.gov). The official site of the National Park Service has links about park geology, sightseeing, plants and animals, Native Americans, and other information.

Index

Picture Credits

Cover Photo: © Craig Aurness/CORBIS
© Tom Bean/CORBIS, 12
© Bettmann/CORBIS, 19
Corel Corporation, 11, 17, 21, 23, 25, 26, 29, 33, 35, 37, 39
© George H. Huey/CORBIS, 7
© Hulton/Archive by Getty Images, 16
Chris Jouan, 9
© Wolfgang Kaehler/CORBIS, 14
PhotoDisc, 40
© Patrick Ward/CORBIS, 30

About the Author

Stuart A. Kallen is the author of more than 150 nonfiction books for children and young adults. He has written on topics ranging from the theory of relativity to rock-and-roll history to life on the American frontier. In addition, Mr. Kallen has written award-winning children's videos and television scripts. In his spare time, Stuart A. Kallen is a singer/songwriter/guitarist in San Diego, California.